Tiny-Spiny Animals

Sea Urchins

Lola M. Schaefer

Heinemann Library
Chicago, Illinois

Customer Service 888-454-2279
Visit our website at www.heinemannlibrary.com

Designed by Sue Emerson, Heinemann Library; Page layout by Que-Net Media
Printed and bound in the United States by Lake Book Manufacturing, Inc.
Photo research by Scott Braut

08 07 06 05 04
10 9 8 7 6 5 4 3 2 1

Library of Congress Cataloging-in-Publication Data
Schaefer, Lola M., 1950-
   Sea urchins / Lola M. Schaefer.
      v. cm. – (Tiny-spiny animals)
Contents: What are sea urchins? -- Where do sea urchins live? – What do sea urchins look like? – What do sea urchins feel like? – How do sea urchins use their spines? – How big are sea urchins? – How do sea urchins move? – What do sea urchins eat? – Where do new sea urchins come from?
   ISBN 1-4034-3245-7 (HC), ISBN 1-4034-3330-5 (Pbk.)
   1. Sea urchins–Juvenile literature. [1. Sea urchins.] I. Title.
   QL384.E2S3 2003
   593.9'5–dc21

                                        2003002074

Acknowledgments
The author and publishers are grateful to the following for permission to reproduce copyright material:
Title page, p. 9 Gilbert S. Grant/Photo Researchers, Inc.; p. 4 Richard Herrmann/Visuals Unlimited; p. 5 R. J. Erwin/Photo Researchers, Inc.; p. 6 Dave B. Fleetham/Visuals Unlimited; p. 7 David Hosking/FLPA; p. 8L Brandon D. Cole/Corbis; pp. 8r, 14r, 15r Corbis; p. 10 Gregory Ochocki/Photo Researchers, Inc.; p. 11l Morton Beebee/Corbis; p. 11r Amos Nachoum/Corbis; p. 12 Robert Yin/Corbis; p. 13 Fred McConnaughey/Photo Researchers, Inc.; p. 14l Phil Degginger/Animals Animals; p. 15l Fred Bavendam/Minden Pictures; p. 16 Biophoto Associates/Photo Researchers, Inc.; pp. 17, 18 David Hall/Photo Researchers, Inc.; pp. 19, 22, 24 D. P. Wilson/FLPA; p. 20 P. Parks/OSF/Animals Animals; p. 21 Andrew J. Martinez/Photo Researchers, Inc.; p. 23 (row 1, L-R) Corbis, R. J. Erwin/Photo Researchers, Inc.; (row 2, L-R) Jeff Rotman/Photo Researchers, Inc., Dave B. Fleetham/Visuals Unlimited, Biophoto Associates/Photo Researchers, Inc.; (row 3) P. Parks/OSF/Animals Animals; back cover (L-R) D. P. Wilson/FLPA, Dave B. Fleetham/Visuals Unlimited

Cover photograph by Randy Morse/Animals Animals

Every effort has been made to contact copyright holders of any material reproduced in this book. Any omissions will be rectified in subsequent printings if notice is given to the publisher.

Special thanks to our advisory panel for their help in the preparation of this book:

Alice Bethke, Library Consultant
Palo Alto, CA

Eileen Day, Preschool Teacher
Chicago, Illinois

Kathleen Gilbert,
Second Grade Teacher
Round Rock, TX

Sandra Gilbert,
Library Media Specialist
Fiest Elementary School
Houston, TX

Jan Gobeille, Kindergarten Teacher
Garfield Elementary
Oakland, CA

Angela Leeper,
Educational Consultant
Wake Forest, NC

Some words are shown in bold, **like this.**
You can find them in the picture glossary on page 23.

Contents

What Are Sea Urchins?

Sea urchins are animals without bones.

They are **invertebrates**.

test

Sea urchins have a hard shell on the outside.

This shell is called a **test**.

Where Do Sea Urchins Live?

All sea urchins live in the ocean.

Most live in deep water.

Some sea urchins live in
shallow water.

They hide between rocks.

What Do Sea Urchins Look Like?

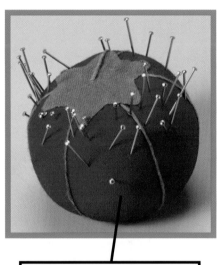

pincushion

Sea urchins look like **pincushions.**

They can be red, purple, green, or black.

spines

Sea urchin **tests** are round.

They are covered with pointy **spines.**

9

What Do Sea Urchins Feel Like?

Sea urchins feel prickly.

Their **spines** are pointy.

People can touch some sea urchins.

Some are too sharp to touch!

How Do Sea Urchins Use Their Spines?

Sea urchins use their **spines** to stay safe.

Their pointy spines keep enemies away.

They use their spines to help them move.

Their spines help them crawl.

How Big Are Sea Urchins?

Some sea urchins are small.

They can be as small as a tennis ball.

Some sea urchins grow to be big.

They can be as big as a soccer ball.

How Do Sea Urchins Move?

tube feet

Sea urchins move very slowly.

They walk on tiny **tube feet**.

Sea urchins also use their **spines** to move.

They move by wiggling their spines.

What Do
Sea Urchins Eat?

Sea urchins eat **kelp**.

They eat kelp as they crawl over it.

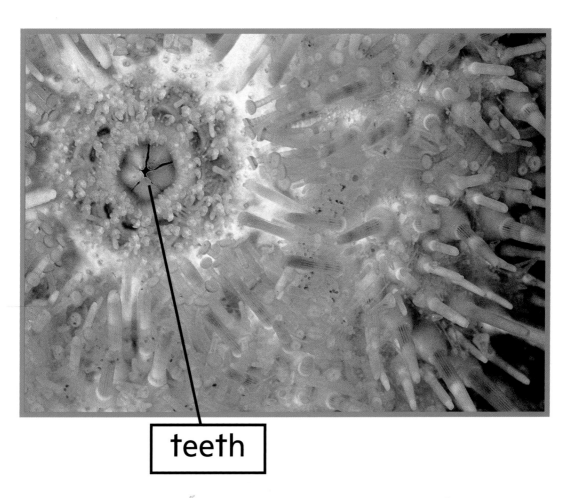

teeth

Sea urchins' mouths are on the bottom of their **tests.**

They have five teeth in their mouths.

Where Do New Sea Urchins Come From?

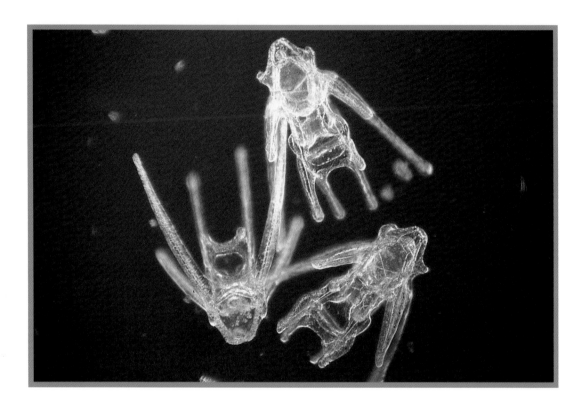

Female sea urchins lay eggs.

Baby sea urchins called **larvae** come out of the eggs.

Later, the larvae change.

They become sea urchins with **spines.**

Quiz

What are these sea urchin parts?

Can you find them in the book?

Look for the answers on page 24.

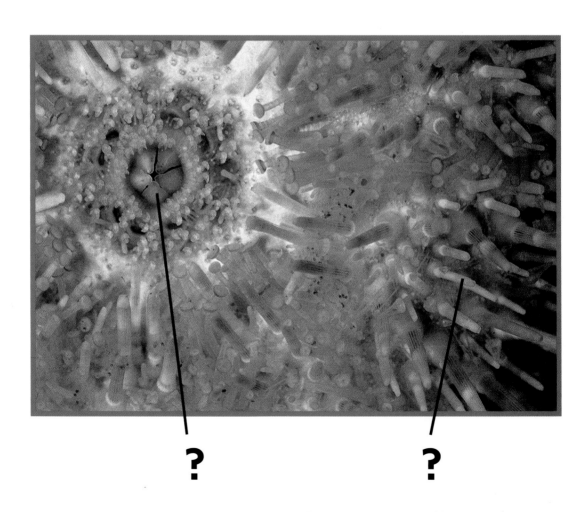

?   ?

Picture Glossary

invertebrate
(in-VUR-tuh-brate)
page 4

pincushion
page 8

test
pages 5, 9, 19

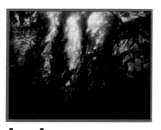

kelp
page 18

spine
pages 9, 10, 12,
13, 17, 21

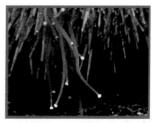

tube feet
page 16

larvae
pages 20, 21

Note to Parents and Teachers

Reading for information is an important part of a child's literacy development. Learning begins with a question about something. Help children think of themselves as investigators and researchers by encouraging their questions about the world around them. Each chapter in this book begins with a question. Read the question together. Look at the pictures. Talk about what you think the answer might be. Then read the text to find out if your predictions were correct. Think of other questions you could ask about the topic, and discuss where you might find the answers.

! CAUTION: Remind children that it is not a good idea to handle wild animals. Children should wash their hands with soap and water after they touch any animal.

Index

Answers to quiz on page 22

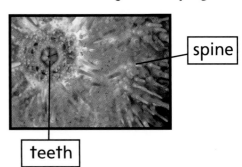

spine

teeth